"Instagram Kingdom"

Building a Brand and Making
On Instagram

by

Mohammad Asif

Disclaimer

This book has been written for the purpose of sharing information only. This book has been carefully written to ensure its accuracy and comprehensiveness. However, there may be some grammatical or substance errors. Additionally, this book only gives information as to the time of publication. As a result, this book has to be regarded as a reference rather than as the final word.

The purpose of this book is to educate. The author and publisher shall not be liable for any mistakes or omissions. The author and publisher shall not be liable or responsible to any person or entity regarding any loss or damage caused or said to have been caused directly or indirectly by this book.

Mohammad Asif

Was born in Kolkata, India. He is a Digital Entrepreneur, Digital Creator, Social Media Influencer and Mentor. After completing his graduation from University of Calcutta, he started his journey in the Digital Era as a Digital Creator and Influencer with an aim to give a new hope to people and make them feel happy and inspired through his content on Instagram. Meanwhile, he was also doing a professional course (CMA), but after a year, he started showing interest in digital entrepreneurship, online business and brand and personality building, accordingly he started to explore these more deeply. After a deep research and learning he then began his career as a Digital

Entrepreneur and Mentor. Now he is guiding and helping people with his learning and experience. Today he is living with only one aim, to help and empower every individual by sharing whatever he has learned during his journey.

"Building a Brand on Instagram"

What does it mean to build a brand?

Building a brand is the process of creating and establishing a unique identity and image for your business or organization. This can include developing a mission statement, creating a logo and visual identity, and consistently communicating your values and messaging to your target audience. Developing a strong brand can help increase customer loyalty, differentiate you from competitors, and ultimately drive business growth.

Table of Contents

CHAPTER 1
"Introduction: The Power of Instagram for Building a Brand"

The "Power of Instagram for Building a Brand" is the first chapter of the book, which aims to provide readers with an overview of the power and potential of Instagram as a platform for building a brand and making money. The chapter would introduce the topic by discussing the importance of social media in today's digital landscape and the significant role that Instagram plays in it.

It sets the stage for the rest of the book by highlighting the power of Instagram as a tool for building a brand. It likely includes statistics and examples of businesses and individuals who have successfully leveraged Instagram to grow their brand and increase their revenue. The introduction may also touch on the unique features and capabilities of Instagram that make it an especially effective platform for these purposes, such as its visual nature, engagement-boosting tools, and large user base. Additionally, it may also mention about the goal of the book, which is to provide readers with a comprehensive guide on how to create a profitable and sustainable Instagram presence.

It could be more detailed by providing a clear overview of the book's content, including the key topics that will be covered in each chapter, and what the readers will learn from reading the book. It could also give an overview of the current state of Instagram as a social media platform, and how it has evolved over the years to become a powerful tool for businesses and individuals to connect with their audience and make money. Some examples of how Instagram has been used effectively in the past to build a brand and make money could also be included.

It could also discuss the importance of having a strong Instagram presence in today's digital landscape. It could emphasize the benefits of using Instagram for business, such as increasing brand awareness, generating leads and sales, and building a community of loyal customers. The introduction could also mention that the book is designed to be a step-by-step guide and is meant to be accessible to readers of all skill levels, whether they are just starting out on Instagram or are looking to take their existing presence to the next level.

Overall, the introduction is meant to provide the readers with a clear understanding of the book's purpose, its main topics and how it will be beneficial for them. It is meant to create a sense of anticipation and interest that will encourage the readers to keep reading and learn more about how to build a successful Instagram presence.

CHAPTER 2
"Setting Up Your Instagram Profile for Success"

This chapter would provide readers with a step-by-step guide for creating an Instagram profile that is optimized for success. It would cover a range of topics, including how to choose the right username and profile picture, how to write an engaging bio, and how to create a visually appealing feed. The chapter would also cover how to use Instagram's features to connect with your audience, and how to measure the performance of your profile.

The chapter would begin by providing tips on how to choose a username that is easy to remember and represents your brand, as well as how to select a profile picture that is visually appealing and represents your brand. It would also cover the importance of using the same username across all of your social media accounts to make it easy for people to find and follow you.

Next, it would provide tips on how to write a bio that accurately represents your brand and entices people to follow you. It would include information on how to use keywords, hashtags, and emojis to make your bio more discoverable, as well as how to use Instagram's bio links feature to drive traffic to other social media accounts or your websites.

The chapter would then cover the importance of using relevant keywords in your bio, captions, and hashtags to make your profile more discoverable to potential followers. It would also include information on how to use Instagram's business profile features to add contact information and access insights.

The chapter would then provide tips on how to use Instagram's editing features to enhance your photos and videos, and how to use a consistent color scheme and aesthetic to make your profile stand out. It would also include information on how to plan and schedule your posts to ensure that your profile is active and engaging at all times.

The chapter would then cover how to utilize Instagram's features such as IGTV, Reels and Instagram Live to build your brand and connect with your audience. It would include information on how to create engaging content for IGTV and Reels, and how to use Instagram Live to connect with your followers in real-time.

Lastly, the chapter would cover how to use Instagram's insights feature to measure the performance of your profile, understand your audience, and make data-driven decisions.

1. Username: A username, also known as a handle, is the name that is used to identify an individual or a business on Instagram. It appears in the profile URL and can be used to find an account in search results (See the example in figure. 1).

Figure. 1: Example of Username

a. Choosing a username: When choosing a username, it's important to make it unique, recognizable, and easy to remember. For a business, it's best to use the business name or a variation of it as the username.

b. Changing the username: It's possible to change the username at any time by going to the profile settings and updating it.

c. Consistency: To maintain consistency across all platforms and to build a recognizable and reliable brand image, it's important to use the same username across all social media platforms.

d. Usernames for business account: For a business account, it's best to use the business name or a variation of it as the username. This will make it easy for customers to find the account and increase brand recognition (See the example in figure. 2).

e. Length: The maximum length of a username on Instagram is 30 characters, so it's important to keep it short and simple.

Figure. 2: Example of Username for business account

2. Profile Picture: A profile picture is an image that represents an individual or a business on Instagram. It is the main visual representation of an account, and it appears on the profile, in search results, and next to comments and posts.

1. Choosing a profile picture: The profile picture should be an image that accurately represents the individual or business and is easily recognizable. It could be a logo, a headshot, or a product image. It should be visually appealing, high-resolution, and properly cropped to fit the circular frame.

2. Consistency: It's important to maintain consistency across all the platforms and keep the same profile picture to build a recognizable and reliable brand image.

3. Profile picture size: The recommended size for a profile picture on Instagram is 110 x 110 pixels (or 1:1 aspect ratio), which will ensure that the image looks clear and crisp when displayed on the platform.

4. Changing the profile picture: It is possible to change the profile picture at any time by going to the profile settings and uploading a new image.

5. **Profile picture for business account:** For a business account, using a logo or a product image as a profile picture can help customers quickly identify the business and increase brand recognition.

3. Bio: A bio is a short written description of an individual or a business on Instagram. It appears on the profile, under the profile picture and is one of the first things a user sees when visiting an Instagram profile (See the example in figure. 3).

Figure. 3: Example of Bio

18

a. Writing a bio: A bio should be a concise, but accurate description of the individual or business, and should include relevant keywords to make the profile more searchable. It should also include a call-to-action, such as a link to a website or a specific post, to encourage users to engage with the account.

b. Length: An Instagram bio is limited to 150 characters, so it's important to be concise and make the most of the limited space.

c. Bio for business account: For a business account, the bio should include a brief overview of the products or services offered, and the mission statement or brand values. It should also include contact information such as an email address, phone number, or website link to make it easy for potential customers to get in touch (See the example in figure. 4).

d. Emoji's: Instagram bios support emojis, so it's possible to use them to make the bio more attractive and stand out.

e. Editing the bio: The bio can be edited at any time by going to the profile settings and updating the text.

Figure. 4: Example of Username for business account

4. Contact Information: Contact information is the information that makes it easy for people to get in touch with an individual or a business on Instagram.

a. Types of contact information: Contact information can include an email address, phone number, website link, or physical address. It is usually included in the bio section of an Instagram profile, so it is easily accessible to users.

b. Bio for business account: For a business account, it's important to include contact information in the bio, such as an email address, phone number, or website link, to make it easy for potential customers to get in touch.

c. Instagram direct message (DM): Instagram also allows users to send direct messages (DMs) to other users, so it's possible to use this feature to provide customer service and respond to inquiries.

d. Contact button: Instagram also has a feature that allows business accounts to add a "Contact" button to their profile, it can be linked to an email address, phone number, or physical address, and users can easily reach out through the app (See the example in figure. 5).

e. Linking to other platforms: It's possible to include links to other platforms such as Twitter, Facebook, or LinkedIn in the bio or in the contact button, to make it easy for users to connect with the account on other platforms.

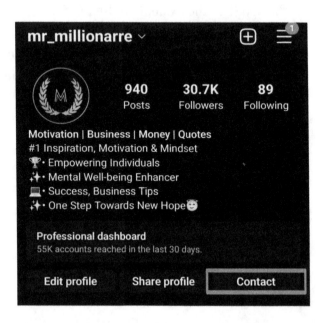

Figure. 5: Example of Contact Button

5. Profile Content: Profile content refers to the images, videos, and written content that is shared on an Instagram profile.

a. Types of content: Profile content can include images, videos, IGTV, Reels, IG stories, and live videos. Each type of content can be used in different ways to showcase different aspects of an individual or a business, such as product demonstrations, behind-the-scenes footage, or customer testimonials.

b. Quality of content: Profile content should be high-quality and visually appealing. It should be well-lit, in focus, and properly cropped. It should also align with the brand's aesthetic and messaging.

c. Consistency: Profile content should be consistent in terms of branding, tone, and visual aesthetic, in order to build a recognizable and reliable brand image.

d. Frequency of posting: Profile content should be posted regularly to keep the account active and engaging.

e. Using Instagram features: Instagram features such as hashtags, polls, questions, and location tags can be used to increase engagement and reach.

f. Profile content for business account: For a business account, profile content should showcase the products or services offered, and provide insight into the brand's mission and values.

6. Instagram Business Account: An Instagram business account is a type of Instagram account that is intended for use by businesses, brands, and organizations. It offers a set of tools and features that are specifically designed for businesses and enables them to promote their products or services, increase brand awareness and track the performance of their Instagram marketing campaigns.

a. Features: Instagram business accounts have access to additional features such as Instagram Insights, which provides analytics and metrics on account performance, and the ability to add a "Contact" button to the profile, which allows users to easily get in touch with the business. They can also access shopping features, promoted posts and Instagram shopping.

b. Instagram Insights: Instagram Insights provides metrics on account performance, such as engagement, reach, and audience growth. It also includes data on audience demographics, such as age, gender, and location, which can be used to inform content and targeting strategies (See the example in figure. 6).

c. Contact button: A contact button allows users to easily get in touch with the business by sending a message or making a phone call directly from the Instagram app (See the example in figure. 5).

d. Shopping feature: Instagram shopping feature allows businesses to tag products in their posts and stories, allowing users to view product details and purchase directly from the app.

e. Promoted posts: Instagram business accounts can promote their posts to reach a larger audience and gain more visibility for their products or services.

f. Advertise: Instagram business accounts can also create and manage Instagram ads through Facebook Ads Manager.

Figure. 6: Example of Insight

7. Consistency: Consistency refers to the degree to which an individual or a business is able to maintain a consistent image, message, and overall aesthetic across all platforms and channels. In the context of Instagram, consistency refers to maintaining a consistent image, message, and overall aesthetic across all posts, stories, IGTV, Reels, and other features.

a. Branding: Consistency in branding refers to maintaining the same visual elements, such as logos, color schemes, and typography, across all posts and stories. This creates a recognizable and reliable brand image.

b. Tone: Consistency in tone refers to maintaining the same tone of voice and messaging across all posts and stories. This helps to create a strong and cohesive brand voice.

c. Posting schedule: Consistency in posting schedule refers to maintaining a regular posting schedule, so that followers know when to expect new content.

d. Aesthetic: Consistency in aesthetic refers to maintaining a consistent visual style across all posts and stories. This includes things like composition, lighting, and color palette.

e. Audience engagement: Consistency in audience engagement refers to maintaining regular interactions with followers, such as responding to comments and messages, to build a loyal following.

Overall, this chapter would provide readers with a comprehensive guide to setting up and optimizing an Instagram profile for success. It would cover everything from choosing the right username and profile picture to creating a consistent and visually appealing feed, and utilizing Instagram's features to connect with your audience and build your brand. The chapter would also include tips and best practices for measuring the performance of your profile and making data-driven decisions.

CHAPTER 3
"Finding Your Niche: Defining Your Target Audience"

It would provide readers with a guide for identifying and targeting a specific audience on Instagram. It would cover the importance of having a well-defined target audience in order to create content that resonates with them and ultimately drive engagement and sales.

The chapter would begin by explaining the concept of niche and why it is important in today's digital landscape. It would provide examples of successful niche accounts on Instagram and the reasons why they have been successful.

Next, the chapter would provide tips on how to identify and research your target audience. It would include information on how to use Instagram's insights feature to understand your current audience, as well as how to conduct market research to identify potential new target audiences.

The chapter would include information on how to gather information on their demographics, interests, pain points, and goals, and how to use this information to create content that speaks directly to them.

The chapter would also cover how to use Instagram's targeting features to reach your target audience. It would include information on how to use Instagram's targeting options, such as location, interests, behaviors, and demographics, to reach the right people at the right time.

Lastly, the chapter would provide tips on how to continue to refine and evolve your target audience over time. It would include information on how to use Instagram's insights feature to track your audience's engagement and growth, and how to use this information to make data-driven decisions about your content and targeting strategies.

1. Niche: A niche refers to a specific segment of a market that is characterized by a specific set of needs, wants, and characteristics. In the context of Instagram, a niche refers to a specific topic, theme, or industry that an account focuses on and targets. By identifying a niche and targeting a specific audience, an account is able to create content that is more relevant, engaging, and likely to convert its audience into customers (See the example in figure. 7).

Figure. 7: Example of Niches

a. **Finding a niche:** Finding a niche involves researching the market and identifying areas of interest, passion, and expertise. Identifying a specific topic, theme or industry that is not overly saturated, that the account can create unique and valuable content for.

b. **Defining the target audience:** Once a niche is identified, the target audience can be defined by identifying the characteristics, behaviors, and needs of the people who are interested in that niche.

c. Creating content: Creating content that is relevant, engaging and valuable for the target audience, and aligns with the niche chosen.

d. Building a community: Building a community around the niche and engaging with the target audience, by replying to comments and messages, hosting giveaways and contests, and creating engagement-based content.

e. Monetizing: Monetizing the account by promoting relevant products, services, or by collaborating with brands that align with the niche.

2. Identifying the target audience: Identifying the target audience refers to the process of understanding the characteristics and needs of the individuals or groups of people that a business or brand wants to reach and engage with on Instagram. This information is used to inform content, targeting, and engagement strategies, and to measure the success of Instagram marketing campaigns.

a. Demographics: Demographics such as age, gender, location, education, income, and occupation can be used to identify the target audience.

b. Interests: Understanding the interests of the target audience, such as hobbies, passions, and lifestyle, can help to inform content strategies and tailor messaging.

c. Behavior: Understanding how the target audience behaves online and offline, such as their online habits, purchase behavior, and brand loyalty, can help to inform targeting strategies and engagement.

d. Personas: Creating buyer personas, which are fictional representations of the target audience, can help to visualize and understand the target audience better.

e. Research: Research methods such as surveys, focus groups, and social listening can be used to gather information about the target audience.

f. Use of analytics: Use of analytics tools such as Instagram Insights can be used to track the performance of posts, stories, IGTV, Reels, and other features, and analyze metrics such as engagement, reach, and audience demographics.

3. Developing personas: Developing personas refers to the process of creating fictional representations of the target audience in order to better understand their characteristics, needs, and behaviors. Personas are useful for creating targeted and effective marketing campaigns, and to help guide the development of products and services.

a. Characteristics: Personas should include information about the target audience's demographics, such as age, gender, location, education, income, and occupation. They should also include information about the target audience's interests, hobbies, passions, and lifestyle.

b. Goals and pain points: Personas should also include information about the target audience's goals, such as what they hope to achieve or what problems they are trying to solve. They should also include information about the target audience's pain points, such as what they are struggling with or what they are dissatisfied with.

c. Motivations and decision-making process: Personas should also include information about the target audience's motivations, such as what drives them to take action, and the decision-making process they go through when considering products or services.

d. Use of research: Personas should be based on research, such as surveys, focus groups, and social listening, to ensure that they are accurate and reflective of the target audience.

e. Use in marketing: Personas can be used in marketing campaigns to create targeted and effective messaging, and to guide the development of products and services that meet the needs of the target audience.

4. Segmentation: Segmentation refers to the process of dividing a target audience into smaller groups based on specific characteristics or criteria, such as demographics, interests, behavior, or purchase history. The goal of segmentation is to create smaller, more specific target groups that can be reached with tailored messaging and more effective marketing campaigns.

a. Demographics: Segmentation based on demographics such as age, gender, location, education, income, and occupation can be used to reach specific groups of people.

b. Interests: Segmentation based on interests, such as hobbies, passions, and lifestyle, can be used to reach specific groups of people who have similar interests.

c. Behavior: Segmentation based on behavior, such as online habits, purchase behavior, and brand loyalty, can be used to reach specific groups of people who exhibit similar behaviors.

d. Purchase history: Segmentation based on purchase history, such as previous purchases or abandoned shopping carts, can be used to target specific groups of people who have shown a likelihood to buy.

e. Use of analytics: Analytics tools such as Instagram Insights can be used to track the performance of posts, stories, IGTV, Reels, and other features and analyze metrics such as engagement, reach, and audience demographics, and then can be used to segment the audience.

f. Use in marketing: Segmentation can be used in marketing campaigns to create more targeted and effective messaging and to create more effective targeting strategies.

5.   Analyzing   competitors: Analyzing competitors refers to the process of studying the strategies, tactics, and performance of other brands or businesses in the same industry or niche as yours on Instagram. The goal of analyzing competitors is to identify their strengths and weaknesses, and to gain insights that can inform your own Instagram marketing strategy.

a. Research: Researching competitors can include studying their Instagram profiles, posts, stories, IGTV, Reels, and other features, as well as their overall online presence and marketing strategies.

b. Identify strengths and weaknesses: By researching competitors, you can identify their strengths, such as what they do well, and their weaknesses, such as what they don't do well. This can help you to understand how to improve your own Instagram marketing strategy.

c. Audience engagement: Analyze how your competitors are engaging with their audience, such as responding to comments and messages, and how they are using Instagram features such as hashtags, polls, questions, and location tags.

d. Use of analytics: Use of analytics tools such as Instagram Insights can be used to track the performance of competitors' posts, stories, IGTV, Reels, and other features, and analyze metrics such as engagement, reach, and audience demographics.

e. Use in marketing: Analyzing competitors can be used to inform your own Instagram marketing strategy, such as identifying opportunities to differentiate your brand or products, and creating targeted and effective messaging.

6. Identifying the pain points: Identifying the pain points refers to the process of identifying the specific problems, needs, or issues that a target audience faces in their lives or in the use of a product or service. It is an important aspect of audience insights and can help businesses tailor their content, messaging, and strategies to better address the needs of their target audience.

a. Research: Research methods such as surveys, focus groups, and social listening can be used to gather information about the target audience's pain points.

b. Use of analytics: Use of analytics tools such as Instagram Insights can be used to track the performance of posts, stories, IGTV, Reels, and other features, and analyze metrics such as engagement, reach, and audience demographics. This can help to identify pain points related to audience engagement, such as lack of engagement or low reach.

c. Use in product development: Identifying pain points can be used to inform the development of products or services that address specific problems and provide solutions for the target audience.

d. Use in marketing: Identifying pain points can be used to inform marketing campaigns, such as creating targeted and effective messaging that addresses specific problems and provides solutions for the target audience.

7. Measuring Success: Measuring success refers to the process of evaluating the performance and effectiveness of an Instagram marketing campaign or strategy, in order to identify areas of improvement and make data-driven decisions.

a. Setting goals: Setting specific, measurable, achievable, relevant, and time-bound (SMART) goals is the first step in measuring success. These goals should align with the overall objectives of the campaign or strategy.

b. Use of analytics: Use of analytics tools such as Instagram Insights can be used to track the performance of posts, stories, IGTV, Reels, and other features, and analyze metrics such as engagement, reach, and audience demographics.

c. Key performance indicators (KPIs): Identifying key performance indicators (KPIs) that align with the SMART goals and objectives of the campaign, such as website traffic, conversion rates, and return on investment (ROI) can be used to measure the success of a campaign.

d. Benchmarking: Comparing the performance of your account to that of your competitors, industry averages or previous campaigns, can help to understand your performance in relation to others and identify areas of improvement.

e. Use in future strategy: By measuring the success of a campaign or strategy, businesses and brands can use the information to make data-driven decisions and improve future campaigns.

Overall, the goal of this chapter is to provide readers with a comprehensive guide for identifying and targeting a specific audience on Instagram. By understanding their target audience, readers will be able to create content that resonates with them and ultimately drive engagement and sales.

CHAPTER 4
"Creating Engaging Content: Tips and Tricks"

This chapter would provide readers with a guide for creating content that resonates with their target audience and drives engagement on Instagram. It would cover a range of topics, including how to create visually appealing content, how to use Instagram's editing tools, and how to come up with new content ideas.

The chapter would begin by providing tips on how to create visually appealing content, such as using high-quality images and videos, using a consistent aesthetic, and incorporating Instagram's editing tools. It would also cover the importance of using a consistent aesthetic to make your content easily recognizable to your target audience.

Next, The chapter would provide tips on how to create different types of content, such as carousels, IGTV, Instagram Reels and Instagram Live. It would include information on how to create engaging content for each of these formats, and how to use them to connect with your audience in different ways.

The chapter would then cover how to come up with new content ideas, such as using Instagram's trends and hashtags, creating a content calendar and repurposing old content. It would also include tips on how to use Instagram's analytics to understand what type of content resonates with your audience and how to adjust your content strategy accordingly.

Lastly, the chapter would provide tips on how to measure the performance of your content, such as using Instagram's analytics, tracking engagement, and monitoring comments. It would also include best practices for how to respond to comments and feedback, and how to use this information to improve your content strategy over time.

1. Types of content: Instagram offers a variety of content formats that can be used to engage and connect with followers. The different types of content include:

a. Photos: Photos are the most basic form of content on Instagram, and can be used to showcase products, services, or behind-the-scenes content.

b. Videos: Videos can be used to showcase products, services, behind-the-scenes content, or to create a more immersive experience for followers. Instagram supports videos up to 60 seconds in the feed (Reels) and up to 10 minutes in IGTV.

c. IGTV: IGTV is a long-form video feature that allows users to upload videos up to 60 minutes in length. IGTV can be used to create a more in-depth and engaging experience for followers.

d. Stories: Stories are short, temporary videos or photos that disappear after 24 hours. Stories can be used to showcase behind-the-scenes content, promote products, or create a sense of exclusivity.

e. Reels: Reels are short, entertaining videos that are similar to TikTok. They can be used to showcase products, services, or to create a more engaging and immersive experience for followers.

f. Live: Instagram Live is a feature that allows users to stream live video to their followers. Live videos can be used to create a sense of exclusivity and to connect with followers in real-time.

g. Carousel: Carousel is a feature that allows users to upload multiple photos or videos in a single post. Carousel can be used to showcase different products, services, or to create a more immersive experience for followers.

2. Visual storytelling: Visual storytelling refers to the use of visual elements, such as images and videos, to tell a story or convey a message on Instagram. It is a way to create emotional connections with the audience and make the content more engaging and memorable.

a. Showcasing products or services: Visual storytelling can be used to showcase products or services in a creative and engaging way, by telling a story about the product or service, and how it can benefit the customer.

b. Creating a brand story: Visual storytelling can be used to create a brand story, by sharing the values, mission, and personality of the brand, and how it relates to the customer.

c. Building emotional connections: Visual storytelling can be used to build emotional connections with the audience, by evoking emotions such as happiness, nostalgia, or inspiration.

d. Creating immersive experiences: Visual storytelling can be used to create immersive experiences for the audience, by using a combination of images, videos, and captions to create a sense of being there.

e. Consistency: It is important to maintain consistency in visual storytelling, by using a consistent visual style, message, and overall aesthetic across all posts, stories, IGTV, Reels, and other features.

f. Use of analytics: Use of analytics tools such as Instagram Insights can be used to track the performance of posts, stories, IGTV, Reels, and other features, and analyze metrics such as engagement, reach, and audience demographics, to measure the success of visual storytelling (See the example in figure. 8).

Figure. 8: Example of insight as Analytics Tool

3. Caption writing: Caption writing refers to the process of crafting written text to accompany photos or videos on Instagram. The caption should complement the visual content and provide additional context or information about the post.

a. Complementing the visual content: The caption should complement the visual content, by providing additional information, context, or a call to action that relates to the image or video.

b. Using keywords: Captions can include keywords that are relevant to the image or video, which can help the post to be discoverable on Instagram through search and hashtags.

c. Creating engagement: Captions can be used to create engagement by asking questions, starting a conversation, or encouraging followers to share their own experiences or thoughts.

d. Telling a story: Captions can be used to tell a story, by providing background information, behind-the-scenes insights, or personal anecdotes related to the visual content.

e. Call to action: Captions can include a call to action, such as asking followers to visit a website, sign up for a newsletter, or share the post with their own followers.

f. Use of emojis: Captions can include emojis to make them more visually engaging, and to add an emotional tone to the post.

g. Use of hashtags: Captions can include hashtags, which can be used to increase the visibility of the post, and to reach new audiences.

4. Instagram features: Instagram features refer to the various tools and functionalities that Instagram provides for users to create, share, and engage with content on the platform. Some examples of Instagram features include:

a. Filters: Instagram offers a variety of filters that can be applied to photos and videos to enhance the visual appearance and give them a unique look.

b. Stories: Stories are short, temporary videos or photos that disappear after 24 hours. Stories can be used to showcase behind-the-scenes content, promote products, or create a sense of exclusivity.

c. IGTV: IGTV is a long-form video feature that allows users to upload videos up to 60 minutes in length. IGTV can be used to create a more in-depth and engaging experience for followers.

d. Reels: Reels are short, entertaining videos that are similar to TikTok. They can be used to showcase products, services, or to create a more engaging and immersive experience for followers. The aspect ratio for creating any reels is 9:16.

e. Live: Instagram Live is a feature that allows users to stream live video to their followers. Live videos can be used to create a sense of exclusivity and to connect with followers in real-time.

f. Carousel: Carousel is a feature that allows users to upload multiple photos or videos in a single post. Carousel can be used to showcase different products, services, or to create a more immersive experience for followers.

g. IG Shopping: Instagram Shopping allows users to tag products in their posts, stories, IGTV,

Reels, and other features, and make them shoppable, allowing the audience to buy the products directly from the platform.

h. Instagram Insights: Instagram Insights is a feature that provides information on the performance of posts, stories, IGTV, Reels, and other features, and helps to understand the audience, engagement, reach, and other metrics.

5. The use of Influencer: Influencer marketing refers to the use of individuals who have a significant following on social media, particularly on Instagram, to promote products, services, or brands. These individuals, known as "influencers," have built a large and engaged following, and their endorsement of a product or service can be seen as more trustworthy and authentic than traditional advertising.

a. Identifying influencers: Identifying influencers can be done by researching individuals who have a large following in your niche or industry, and who have a strong engagement with their audience.

b. Building relationships: Building relationships with influencers is an important part of influencer marketing, as it allows brands to align with influencers who are a good fit for their products or services, and who have a genuine interest in the brand.

c. Sponsored posts: Sponsored posts are a common form of influencer marketing, in which an influencer is paid to create a post promoting a product or service.

d. Product reviews: Influencers can also be used to create product reviews, in which they test and review a product or service, and share their thoughts with their followers.

e. Collaborations: Influencer marketing can also involve collaborations, in which influencers and brands work together to create content that promotes both the brand and the influencer.

f. Use of analytics: Use of analytics tools such as Instagram Insights can be used to track the performance of influencer's posts, stories, IGTV, Reels, and other features, and analyze metrics such as engagement, reach, and audience demographics, to measure the success of influencer marketing campaigns.

6. Measuring success: Measuring success refers to the process of evaluating the performance and effectiveness of an Instagram marketing campaign or strategy, in order to identify areas of improvement and make data-driven decisions.

a. Setting goals: Setting specific, measurable, achievable, relevant, and time-bound (SMART) goals is the first step in measuring success. These goals should align with the overall objectives of the campaign or strategy.

b. Use of analytics: Use of analytics tools such as Instagram Insights can be used to track the performance of posts, stories, IGTV, Reels, and other features, and analyze metrics such as engagement, reach, and audience demographics.

c. Key performance indicators (KPIs): Identifying key performance indicators (KPIs) that align with the SMART goals and objectives of the campaign, such as website traffic, conversion rates, and return on investment (ROI) can be used to measure the success of a campaign.

d. Benchmarking: Comparing the performance of your account to that of your competitors, industry averages or previous campaigns, can help to understand your performance in relation to others and identify areas of improvement.

e. Use in future strategy: By measuring the success of a campaign or strategy, businesses and brands can use the information to make data-driven decisions and improve future campaigns.

Overall, the goal of this chapter is to provide readers with a comprehensive guide for creating content that resonates with their target audience and drives engagement on Instagram. It would cover everything from creating visually appealing content, using Instagram's editing tools, creating different types of content, coming up with new content ideas, and measuring the performance of your content.

CHAPTER 5
"Utilizing IGTV and Instagram Stories to Connect with Your Audience"

This chapter would provide readers with a guide for using Instagram Stories and IGTV to connect with their target audience in a more engaging and interactive way. It would cover a range of topics, including how to create engaging Instagram Stories, how to use IGTV to create long-form video content, and how to use Instagram's features to drive engagement and grow your audience.

The chapter would begin by providing tips on how to create engaging Instagram Stories, and using hashtags and location tags to increase discoverability. It would also cover the importance of using Instagram's features such as polls, quizzes, and questions to increase engagement and drive conversations with your audience.

Next, the chapter would provide tips on how to use IGTV to create long-form video content that resonates with your target audience. It would include information on how to optimize your IGTV videos for maximum engagement, such as using captions, subtitles, and calls-to-action. It would also include examples of how businesses and individuals have used IGTV to create engaging and educational content that has helped them build their brand and connect with their audience.

The chapter would also cover how to use Instagram's features such as Instagram Live, to connect with your audience in real-time. It would provide tips on how to create engaging live content, such as using interactive features like polls and Q&A sessions, and how to promote your live stream in advance to increase viewership.

Lastly, The chapter would cover the importance of analyzing and tracking the performance of your Instagram Stories and IGTV content, using Instagram's analytics and insights features. It would include tips on how to use this data to optimize your content strategy and improve engagement over time.

1. Instagram Stories: Instagram Stories are short, temporary videos or photos that disappear after 24 hours. Stories are a feature that allows users to share behind-the-scenes content, promote products, or create a sense of exclusivity with their followers.

a. Creating content: Instagram Stories can be created using photos or videos, and can be decorated with text, stickers, polls, questions, and location tags.

b. Highlighting: Instagram Stories can be saved and highlighted on the user's profile, allowing them to be viewed even after 24 hours.

c. Swipe-up links: Instagram Stories can include a swipe-up link, which allows users to direct their followers to a website, product page, or other external link.

d. Hashtags: Instagram Stories can include hashtags, which can be used to increase the visibility of the story, and to reach new audiences.

e. Sticker: Instagram Stories can include a variety of stickers, such as polls, questions, location tags, and mentions, which can be used to create engagement and encourage interaction with followers.

f. Analytics: Instagram Insights can be used to track the performance of Instagram Stories, and to analyze metrics such as reach, engagement, and audience demographics.

2. IGTV: IGTV (Instagram TV) is a long-form video feature on Instagram that allows users to upload videos up to 60 minutes in length. IGTV is a stand-alone app and a feature on the Instagram app, which can be accessed through the user's profile or by searching for specific channels.

a. Creating content: IGTV videos can be created using existing videos or by filming directly through the IGTV app. Users can upload videos up to 60 minutes in length, and can also add captions, location tags, and hashtags.

b. Channel: IGTV allows users to create their own channel, where all their videos are grouped together and can be accessed by their followers.

c. Discoverability: IGTV videos can be discovered through the IGTV app or by searching for specific channels, hashtags, or location tags.

d. Vertical videos: IGTV videos are designed to be viewed in a vertical format, which is more natural for mobile devices.

e. Call-to-action: IGTV videos can include a call-to-action, such as asking followers to visit a website, sign up for a newsletter, or share the video with their own followers.

f. Analytics: IGTV offers analytics, which allows users to track the performance of their videos, and analyze metrics such as views, likes, comments, and engagement.

3. Creating content: Creating content refers to the process of producing and publishing images, videos, and written text on Instagram. This can include creating posts, stories, IGTV videos, reels, and other types of content.

a. Planning: Planning is an important part of creating content, as it allows you to set goals, identify target audience, and decide on the type of content you want to create.

b. Visual storytelling: Creating visually engaging content that tells a story or conveys a message is important, as it allows you to create emotional connections with your audience, and make the content more memorable.

c. Caption writing: Captions should complement the visual content, provide additional context or information about the post, use keywords, create engagement, tell a story, include a call to action, use emojis, and include relevant hashtags.

d. Use of Instagram features: Instagram features such as filters, polls, questions, location tags, and hashtags can be used to enhance the visual appearance of the content and increase engagement.

e. Use of analytics: Use of analytics tools such as Instagram Insights can be used to track the performance of the content, and analyze metrics such as engagement, reach, and audience demographics, to measure the success of the content (See the example in figure. 9).

f. Consistency: Consistency is important when creating content, as it helps to maintain the brand image, and create a sense of familiarity with the audience.

Figure. 9: Example of insight as Analytics Tool to tack Reach

4. Measuring success: Measuring success refers to the process of evaluating the performance and effectiveness of an Instagram marketing campaign or strategy, in order to identify areas of improvement and make data-driven decisions.

a. Setting goals: Setting specific, measurable, achievable, relevant, and time-bound (SMART) goals is the first step in measuring success. These goals should align with the overall objectives of the campaign or strategy.

b. Use of analytics: Use of analytics tools such as Instagram Insights can be used to track the performance of posts, stories, IGTV, Reels, and other features, and analyze metrics such as engagement, reach, and audience demographics.

c. Key performance indicators (KPIs): Identifying key performance indicators (KPIs) that align with the SMART goals and objectives of the campaign, such as website traffic, conversion rates, and return on investment (ROI) can be used to measure the success of a campaign.

d. Benchmarking: Comparing the performance of your account to that of your competitors, industry averages or previous campaigns, can help to understand your performance in relation to others and identify areas of improvement.

e. Use in future strategy: By measuring the success of a campaign or strategy, businesses and brands can use the information to make data-driven decisions and improve future campaigns.

5. Cross-promoting: Cross-promoting refers to the practice of promoting a brand, product, or service across multiple social media platforms or channels. The goal of cross-promotion is to increase brand awareness, reach a wider audience, and drive engagement and conversions.

a. Linking accounts: Cross-promotion can involve linking accounts across different social media platforms, such as linking Instagram to Facebook, Twitter, TikTok, or YouTube, which allows users to share content across multiple platforms.

b. Collaborations: Cross-promotion can also involve collaborations with other brands, influencers, or businesses that have a similar target audience. Collaborating with other brands or influencers to create content or campaigns that promote both brands can be an effective way to reach a wider audience.

c. Use of hashtags: Cross-promotion can also involve using relevant hashtags to increase the visibility of the content across different platforms.

d. Linking website: Cross-promotion can also involve linking website, blog, or landing page to the social media profiles, in order to drive more traffic to the website.

e. Use of analytics: Use of analytics tools such as Instagram Insights, Google Analytics, and other third party tools can be used to track the performance of the cross-promotion campaigns, and analyze metrics such as engagement, reach, and audience demographics, to measure the success of the cross-promotion.

Overall, the goal of this chapter is to provide readers with a comprehensive guide for using Instagram Stories and IGTV to connect with their target audience in a more engaging and interactive way. It would cover everything from creating engaging content, using Instagram's features to drive engagement, analyzing and tracking the performance of your content, and best practices for using Instagram stories for e-commerce. By utilizing these features, readers will be able to create a deeper connection with their audience and increase engagement on their Instagram account.

CHAPTER 6
"Maximizing Reach and Engagement: Instagram Ads, Hashtags and Influencer Marketing"

This chapter would provide readers with a guide for increasing reach and engagement on their Instagram account through the use of hashtags, Instagram ads, and influencer marketing. It would cover a range of topics, including how to find and use relevant hashtags, how to create effective Instagram ads, and how to work with influencers to build your brand and reach a larger audience.

The chapter would begin by providing tips on how to find and use relevant hashtags to increase the discoverability of your content. It would include information on how to use Instagram's hashtag suggestion feature, how to find popular hashtags in your niche, and how to use hashtags to reach new audiences.

Next, the chapter would provide tips on how to create effective Instagram ads. It would include information on how to use Instagram's ad targeting options, how to create engaging ad copy and visuals, and how to measure the performance of your ads. It would also cover the different types of Instagram ads such as photo ads, video ads, carousel ads, etc.

The chapter would then cover how to work with influencers to build your brand and reach a larger audience. It would include information on how to find and work with influencers in your niche and how to measure the success of your influencer marketing campaigns.

Lastly, the chapter would provide tips on how to measure the performance of your Instagram account, such as using Instagram's insights feature, tracking engagement and monitoring comments. It would also include best practices for how to respond to comments and feedback, and how to use this information to improve your content strategy over time.

1. Instagram Ads: Instagram Ads are a form of paid advertising on the Instagram platform. Businesses can use Instagram Ads to promote their products, services, or brand to a targeted audience. Instagram ads can appear in several places in the Instagram app like in the feed, stories, IGTV, Reels and Explore.

a. Ad formats: Instagram offers various ad formats such as photo, video, carousel, story, IGTV, and Reels ads. The format of the ad will depend on the objective of the campaign and the message that you want to convey to the audience.

b. Targeting: Instagram allows businesses to target specific audiences based on factors such as demographics, interests, behaviors, and location. This helps to ensure that the ads reach the right people, and increase the chances of success.

c. Ad placements: Instagram Ads can be placed in several places like in the feed, stories, IGTV, Reels and Explore. The placement of the ad will depend on the objective of the campaign, the format of the ad, and the audience that you want to reach.

d. Ad campaigns: Instagram Ads can be created as part of an ad campaign, which allows businesses to set a budget, schedule the ads, and track the performance of the ads over time.

e. Instagram Insights: Instagram Insights can be used to track the performance of Instagram Ads, and to analyze metrics such as views, clicks, conversions, and audience demographics.

f. Ad formats: Instagram offers various ad formats such as photo, video, carousel, story, IGTV, and Reels ads, that can be used to reach a specific audience, to increase brand awareness, and to drive engagement and conversions.

2. Hashtags: Hashtags are a feature on Instagram (and other social media platforms) that allows users to tag their posts with keywords, making them discoverable to other users. When a user clicks on a hashtag, they are taken to a feed of all the public posts that have used that same hashtag.

a. Creating Hashtags: Hashtags can be created by adding the "#" symbol before a word or phrase (e.g. #travel, #photography). When creating hashtags, it's important to make them relevant to the content of the post, and to use keywords that users are likely to search for.

b. Using Hashtags: Hashtags can be added to the caption of a post, as well as in the comments section. It's generally recommended to use a mix of both branded and non-branded hashtags, and to use a maximum of 15-20 hashtags per post (Max Hashtags Limit is 30).

c. Popular hashtags: Popular hashtags are hashtags that are widely used across Instagram, and can help to increase the visibility of the post, and reach new audiences.

d. Branded hashtags: Branded hashtags are hashtags that are specific to a brand or product, and can be used to increase brand awareness, and to track the performance of branded content.

e. Instagram Hashtags: Instagram also provides a feature to follow hashtags, which allows users to see content from multiple accounts using that hashtag in their main feed.

f. Hashtag analytics: Instagram Insights can be used to track the performance of hashtags, and to analyze metrics such as reach, engagement, and audience demographics.

3. Influencer Marketing: Influencer marketing refers to the practice of working with individuals who have a significant following on social media, particularly on Instagram, to promote products, services, or brands. Influencers are individuals who have built a large and engaged following and their endorsement of a product or service can be seen as more trustworthy and authentic than traditional advertising.

a. Identifying influencers: Identifying influencers can be done by researching individuals who have a large following in your niche or industry, and who have a strong engagement with their audience.

b. Building relationships: Building relationships with influencers is an important part of influencer marketing, as it allows brands to align with influencers who are a good fit for their products or services, and who have a genuine interest in the brand.

c. Sponsored posts: Sponsored posts are a common form of influencer marketing, in which an influencer is paid to create a post promoting a product or service.

d. Product reviews: Influencers can also be used to create product reviews, in which they test and review a product or service, and share their thoughts with their followers.

e. Collaborations: Influencer marketing can also involve collaborations, in which influencers and brands work together to create content that promotes both the brand and the influencer.

f. Use of analytics: Use of analytics tools such as Instagram Insights can be used to track the performance of influencer's posts, stories, IGTV, Reels, and other features, and analyze metrics such as engagement, reach, and audience demographics, to measure the success of influencer marketing campaigns (See the example in figure. 10).

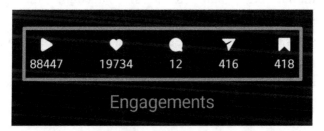

Figure. 10: Example of insight as Analytics Tool to track Engagements

Overall, the goal of this chapter is to provide readers with a comprehensive guide for increasing reach and engagement on their Instagram account through the use of hashtags, Instagram ads, and influencer marketing. By utilizing these strategies, readers will be able to expand their reach, increase their visibility, and ultimately drive more engagement and sales on their Instagram account.

CHAPTER 7
"Monetizing Your Instagram Account: Product Sales, Sponsored Posts and Digital Marketing"

This chapter would provide readers with a guide for monetizing their Instagram account through sponsored posts, digital marketing, and product sales. The chapter would cover a range of topics, including how to work with brands, how to create digital marketing partnerships, and how to sell products through Instagram.

The chapter would begin by providing tips on how to work with brands, such as how to find brands to work with, how to negotiate rates, and how to create engaging sponsored posts that align with your brand and message. It would also cover the importance of disclosing sponsored content in accordance with FTC guidelines.

Next, the chapter would cover how to sell products through Instagram, such as how to use Instagram's shoppable posts feature, how to create an Instagram shop, and how to use Instagram to drive sales to an e-commerce website. It would also cover the best practices for creating an Instagram shop and how to use Instagram's analytics to track sales.

Lastly, the chapter would provide tips on how to measure the performance of your monetization efforts, such as tracking sponsored post performance and tracking product sales. It would also include best practices for optimizing your monetization strategy over time, such as testing different types of sponsored posts and adjusting your pricing and product offerings to better meet the needs of your target audience.

1. Product sales: Product sales refer to the process of selling products or services on Instagram through the use of various features such as Instagram Shopping, Instagram Checkout, and Instagram Live Shopping.

a. Instagram Shopping: Instagram Shopping is a feature that allows businesses to tag products in their posts and stories, and link them directly to the product page on their website. This feature allows customers to view product details, prices, and purchase the product directly from Instagram.

b. **Instagram Checkout:** Instagram Checkout is a feature that allows customers to purchase products directly from Instagram, without leaving the app. This feature is available for eligible businesses in certain countries.

c. **Instagram Live Shopping:** Instagram Live Shopping is a feature that allows businesses to tag products during a live video, and allow customers to purchase the products directly from the live video.

d. **Product catalog:** Product catalog is a feature that allows businesses to upload and manage their products on Instagram, and to tag them in posts and stories.

e. **Instagram Insights:** Instagram Insights can be used to track the performance of the product sales, and to analyze metrics such as views, clicks, and purchases, to measure the success of the product sales on Instagram.

2. Sponsored posts: specifically on Instagram, in which an influencer is paid to create a post promoting a product or service. These posts are labeled as sponsored or paid partnerships, so that the audience is aware that the post is an advertisement.

a. Collaboration with influencers: Sponsored posts are typically created in collaboration with influencers, who have a significant following and engagement on the platform. This allows brands to reach a wider audience and increase brand awareness.

b. Alignment with the influencer's niche: Brands should align with influencers whose niche or industry is related to the brand, in order to ensure that the sponsorship is a good fit and that the audience is interested in the product or service being promoted.

c. Authenticity and transparency: Sponsored posts should be authentic and transparent, as they are viewed as more trustworthy and credible when it comes from the influencer. The influencer should be genuinely interested in the product or service and should disclose the partnership clearly to their followers.

d. Use of analytics: Use of analytics tools such as Instagram Insights can be used to track the performance of sponsored posts, and analyze metrics such as engagement, reach, and audience demographics, to measure the success of the campaign.

3. Influencer marketing: Influencer marketing refers to the practice of working with individuals who have a significant following on social media, particularly on Instagram, to promote products, services, or brands. Influencers are individuals who have built a large and engaged following and their endorsement of a product or service can be seen as more trustworthy and authentic than traditional advertising.

a. Identifying influencers: Identifying influencers can be done by researching individuals who have a large following in your niche or industry, and who have a strong engagement with their audience.

b. Building relationships: Building relationships with influencers is an important part of influencer marketing, as it allows brands to align with influencers who are a good fit for their products or services, and who have a genuine interest in the brand.

c. Sponsored posts: Sponsored posts are a common form of influencer marketing, in which an influencer is paid to create a post promoting a product or service.

d. Product reviews: Influencers can also be used to create product reviews, in which they test and review a product or service, and share their thoughts with their followers.

e. Collaborations: Influencer marketing can also involve collaborations, in which influencers and brands work together to create content that promotes both the brand and the influencer.

f. Use of analytics: Use of analytics tools such as Instagram Insights can be used to track the performance of influencer's posts, stories, IGTV, Reels, and other features, and analyze metrics such as engagement, reach, and audience demographics, to measure the success of influencer marketing campaigns.

4. FTC Guidelines: FTC (Federal Trade Commission) guidelines are a set of rules and regulations established by the United States Federal Trade Commission to ensure that advertising and marketing on social media platforms, such as Instagram, is truthful, not misleading, and not deceptive. These guidelines apply to all forms of social media advertising, including sponsored posts, influencer marketing, and affiliate marketing.

a. Disclosure: FTC guidelines require that any form of paid promotion or sponsorship on social media must be clearly disclosed to the audience. This means that if a post is sponsored or contains affiliate links, it must be clearly labeled as such, usually through the use of hashtags such as #ad or #sponsored.

b. Honesty: FTC guidelines require that all claims made in social media advertising must be truthful and not misleading. Businesses should be able to back up any claims made in their advertising with evidence.

c. Endorsements: FTC guidelines require that any endorsements made in social media advertising must reflect the honest opinions, findings, beliefs, or experiences of the endorser. This means that influencers and other endorsers cannot be paid to say something they do not truly believe.

d. Fairness: FTC guidelines require that all social media advertising must be fair, and cannot be used to take advantage of consumers.

e. Compliance: FTC guidelines require that businesses must comply with all guidelines and regulations, and failure to comply can result in fines, penalties, or legal action.

5. Measuring success: Measuring success refers to the process of evaluating the performance and effectiveness of an Instagram marketing campaign or strategy, in order to identify areas of improvement and make data-driven decisions.

a. Setting goals: Setting specific, measurable, achievable, relevant, and time-bound (SMART) goals is the first step in measuring success. These goals should align with the overall objectives of the campaign or strategy.

b. Use of analytics: Use of analytics tools such as Instagram Insights can be used to track the performance of posts, stories, IGTV, Reels, and other features, and analyze metrics such as engagement, reach, and audience demographics.

c. Key performance indicators (KPIs): Identifying key performance indicators (KPIs) that align with the SMART goals and objectives of the campaign, such as website traffic, conversion rates, and return on investment (ROI) can be used to measure the success of a campaign.

d. Benchmarking: Comparing the performance of your account to that of your competitors, industry averages or previous campaigns, can help to understand your performance in relation to others and identify areas of improvement.

e. Use in future strategy: By measuring the success of a campaign or strategy, businesses and brands can use the information to make data-driven decisions and improve future campaigns.

Overall, the goal of this chapter is to provide readers with a comprehensive guide for monetizing their Instagram account through sponsored posts, digital marketing, and product sales. By utilizing these strategies, readers will be able to monetize their Instagram account and turn their following into a source of income. The chapter would provide readers with the knowledge, tips and best practices to create a sustainable revenue stream through their Instagram account.

CHAPTER 8
"Measuring Your Success and Analyzing Your Audience"

This chapter would provide readers with a guide for measuring the success of their Instagram account and analyzing their target audience. The chapter would cover a range of topics, including how to use Instagram's analytics and insights, how to track engagement, and how to use this information to optimize their Instagram strategy.

The chapter would begin by providing an overview of Instagram's analytics and insights feature and how to use it to track key metrics such as reach, engagement, and follower growth. It would also cover how to use Instagram's analytics to track the performance of individual posts, stories and IGTV videos, and how to use this information to optimize your content strategy.

Next, the chapter would provide tips on how to track engagement on your Instagram account, such as monitoring likes, comments, and direct messages. It would also cover how to use Instagram's analytics to track engagement over time and how to use this information to identify patterns and trends in your audience's behavior.

The chapter would then cover how to use this information to optimize your Instagram strategy, such as how to identify and target new audiences, how to create content that resonates with your audience, and how to use Instagram's features to drive engagement and grow your audience.

Lastly, the chapter would provide tips on how to use Instagram's analytics to monitor the performance of your monetization efforts, such as tracking sponsored post performance and tracking product sales. It would also include best practices for optimizing your monetization strategy over time.

1. Metrics: Metrics are quantitative measures that are used to evaluate the performance of an Instagram account or campaign. These metrics can be used to track the success of an account, and to make data-driven decisions to improve the performance of the account.

Figure. 11: Example of insight to track performance,
Engagement & Reach

a. Engagement: Engagement metrics measure the level of interaction between an account and its followers, such as likes, comments, shares, and direct messages. High engagement is generally seen as a positive indication of the account's popularity and reach (See the example in figure. 11).

b. Reach: Reach metrics measure the number of people who have seen the account's content. This can include metrics such as impressions, views, and unique views (See the example in figure. 11).

c. Audience demographics: Audience demographics metrics provide information about the demographics of the account's followers, such as age, gender, location, and interests.

d. Traffic: Traffic metrics measure the amount of traffic driven to an external website from an Instagram account.

e. Conversions: Conversion metrics measure the number of conversions (such as sales, sign-ups, or form submissions) that occur as a result of an Instagram campaign.

f. Instagram Insights: Instagram Insights is a built-in analytics tool that provides businesses with detailed metrics about their account. Metrics such as engagement, reach, audience demographics, and insights on posts, stories, IGTV, Reels, and other features can be tracked and analyzed.

2. Analytics tools: analyze data about an Instagram account or campaign. These tools can be used to track key performance indicators (KPIs) such as engagement, reach, audience demographics, traffic, and conversions. There are several analytics tools available for Instagram, some of the popular ones include:

a. Instagram Insights: Instagram Insights is a built-in analytics tool that is available to all Instagram business accounts. It provides detailed metrics about the account's performance, such as engagement, reach, audience demographics, and insights on posts, stories, IGTV, Reels, and other features.

b. Hootsuite Insights: Hootsuite Insights is a social media analytics tool that allows businesses to track and analyze data across multiple social media platforms, including Instagram.

c. Sprout Social: Sprout Social is a social media management and analytics tool that allows businesses to track and analyze data across multiple social media platforms, including Instagram.

d. Iconosquare: Iconosquare is an Instagram analytics tool that provides detailed metrics about an account's performance, such as engagement, reach, and audience demographics.

e. Google Analytics: Google Analytics is a web analytics service that can be used to track and analyze data about an Instagram account or campaign (See the example in figure. 12).

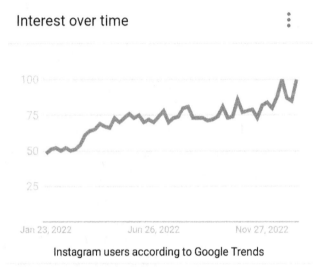

Figure. 12: Example of Google Analytics

3. Third-party tools: Third-party tools are software applications that are developed by companies other than Instagram, that can be used to manage, analyze and optimize an Instagram account or campaign. These tools can be used to track key performance indicators (KPIs) such as engagement, reach, audience demographics, traffic, and conversions, and also provide additional features beyond what is offered by Instagram. Some examples of third-party tools include:

a. Social media management tools: These tools allow businesses to schedule and publish posts, monitor mentions and hashtags, and track analytics across multiple social media platforms including Instagram. Some popular examples include Hootsuite, Sprout Social, Buffer, etc.

b. Instagram scheduling tools: These tools allow businesses to schedule posts in advance, and automatically publish them at a specific time. Some popular examples include Later,Hopper HQ, Facebook Creator Studio, etc.

c. Instagram analytics tools: These tools provide detailed analytics about an Instagram account, such as engagement, reach, audience demographics, and insights on posts, stories, IGTV, Reels, and other features. Some popular examples include Iconosquare, Hootsuite Insights, Sprout Social, etc.

d. Instagram caption writing tools: These tools help businesses to write better captions for their Instagram posts. Some popular examples include Inshot, Canva, Adobe Spark, etc.

4. Audience analysis: characteristics, behaviors, and needs of an Instagram account's target audience. The goal of audience analysis is to gain a better understanding of the people who are most likely to engage with and purchase from the account, in order to tailor the account's content and messaging to better reach and convert them.

a. Demographics: Audience demographics refer to the characteristics of the target audience such as age, gender, location, education level, income level, etc. This data can be obtained from Instagram Insights and third-party analytics tools.

b. Interests: Audience interests refer to the topics, hobbies, and activities that the target audience is interested in. This information can be obtained by analyzing the audience's engagement on the account, such as the types of posts they engage with, the hashtags they use, and the accounts they follow.

c. Pain points: Audience pain points refer to the problems or challenges that the target audience is facing, which the account's products or services can solve. This information can be obtained by conducting surveys, interviews, and focus groups with the target audience.

d. Behavioral analysis: Behavioral analysis refers to the study of how the target audience behaves on Instagram. This includes analyzing the audience's activity on the platform, such as their engagement with the account, the times they are most active, and the types of content they engage with.

e. Competitor analysis: Competitor analysis is the process of researching and analyzing the target audience of the account's competitors. This can provide valuable insights into the target audience's characteristics, behaviors, and needs, and allow the account to tailor its content and messaging to better reach and convert them.

5. A/B testing: A/B testing, also known as split testing, is a method of comparing two or more variations of a marketing element such as a post, a story, a landing page, a subject line, or a call-to-action, to determine which one performs better. A/B testing is commonly used in digital marketing, including on Instagram, to optimize campaigns and improve the performance of an account.

a. Control and variant: In A/B testing, one version of the element is the control, which is the current version or the version that is believed to perform well. The other version(s) are the variants, which are the version(s) that are being tested against the control.

b. Random sampling: A/B testing requires a random sampling of the target audience to be exposed to the control and variant(s). This ensures that the results are statistically significant and not influenced by external factors.

c. Key performance indicators (KPIs): A/B testing is used to measure the performance of the control and variant(s) against specific KPIs, such as engagement, reach, conversions, and click-through rates (CTRs).

d. Data analysis: After the test, the data is analyzed to determine which version performed better. The results can be used to make data-driven decisions to improve the performance of the account.

e. Iteration: A/B testing is an iterative process, meaning that the results of one test can be used to inform the next test. This allows businesses to continuously improve the performance of the account over time.

6. Measuring ROI: Measuring return on investment (ROI) is a method of evaluating the effectiveness of an investment, in this case, an Instagram account or campaign, by comparing the revenue generated to the costs incurred. The goal of measuring ROI is to determine the profitability of an investment and to make data-driven decisions about future investments.

a. Revenue: Revenue refers to the income generated from an Instagram account or campaign, such as sales, sponsorships, and digital marketing.

b. Costs: Costs refer to the expenses incurred from an Instagram account or campaign, such as advertising, content creation, and management.

c. ROI Formula: ROI is calculated by dividing the net profit (revenue - costs) by the costs, and expressing the result as a percentage. (ROI = (Revenue - Costs) / Costs) x 100

d. Tracking: To measure ROI, businesses need to track revenue and costs, which can be done by using tools such as Instagram Insights, Google Analytics, and third-party analytics tools.

e. Analysis: The collected data should be analyzed in order to determine the ROI of an Instagram account or campaign. It is important to track the ROI over time to get a sense of how the investment is performing.

f. Comparison: To make informed decisions, the ROI of an Instagram account or campaign should be compared to industry benchmarks, or to the ROI of other marketing channels.

Overall, the goal of this chapter is to provide readers with a comprehensive guide for measuring the success of their Instagram account and analyzing their target audience. By utilizing the tools and strategies outlined in this chapter, readers will be able to track their progress, identify areas for improvement, and optimize their Instagram strategy to drive engagement and sales.

CHAPTER 9
"Staying Ahead of the Game: Keeping Up with Features and Instagram's Algorithm"

This chapter would provide readers with a guide for staying up-to-date with Instagram's algorithm and features, so they can optimize their Instagram strategy and stay ahead of the competition. The chapter would cover a range of topics, including how Instagram's algorithm works, how to adapt to changes in the algorithm, and how to take advantage of new features as they are released.

The chapter would begin by providing an overview of how Instagram's algorithm works, including the factors that influence reach and engagement. It would also cover how the algorithm has evolved over time and the impact this has had on content distribution. By understanding how the algorithm works, readers can create content that is more likely to be seen and engaged with by their audience.

Next, the chapter would provide tips on how to adapt to changes in the algorithm, such as how to create content that is more likely to be seen and engaged with by the algorithm, and how to use Instagram's features to drive engagement and grow your audience. It would cover best practices for optimizing your Instagram strategy in the face of constant algorithm changes.

The chapter would then cover how to take advantage of new features as they are released, such as how to use Instagram's new features to create more engaging content, how to use Instagram's new features to reach new audiences, and how to use Instagram's new features to drive engagement and grow your audience. By keeping up with new features, readers can stay ahead of the competition and use Instagram's features to their advantage.

Lastly, the chapter would provide tips on how to stay up-to-date with Instagram's algorithm and features, such as following Instagram's official blog, staying current with industry news and trends, and experimenting with new features to see what works best for their audience.

1. Instagram features: Instagram features refer to the various tools and functionalities that Instagram provides for users to create, share, and engage with content on the platform. Some examples of Instagram features include:

a. Filters: Instagram offers a variety of filters that can be applied to photos and videos to enhance the visual appearance and give them a unique look.

b. Stories: Stories are short, temporary videos or photos that disappear after 24 hours. Stories can be used to showcase behind-the-scenes content, promote products, or create a sense of exclusivity.

c. IGTV: IGTV is a long-form video feature that allows users to upload videos up to 60 minutes in length. IGTV can be used to create a more in-depth and engaging experience for followers.

d. Reels: Reels are short, entertaining videos that are similar to TikTok. They can be used to showcase products, services, or to create a more engaging and immersive experience for followers. The aspect ratio for creating any reels is 9:16.

e. Live: Instagram Live is a feature that allows users to stream live video to their followers. Live videos can be used to create a sense of exclusivity and to connect with followers in real-time.

97

f. Carousel: Carousel is a feature that allows users to upload multiple photos or videos in a single post. Carousel can be used to showcase different products, services, or to create a more immersive experience for followers.

g. IG Shopping: Instagram Shopping allows users to tag products in their posts, stories, IGTV, Reels, and other features, and make them shoppable, allowing the audience to buy the products directly from the platform.

h. Instagram Insights: Instagram Insights is a feature that provides information on the performance of posts, stories, IGTV, Reels, and other features, and helps to understand the audience, engagement, reach, and other metrics.

2. Instagram algorithm: The Instagram algorithm is a set of rules and calculations that determine the order in which content is presented to users on the platform. The algorithm is designed to show users the content that they are most likely to be interested in, based on their engagement history, interests, and behavior on the platform. The algorithm is constantly evolving, and businesses need to stay up-to-date with the latest changes in order to optimize their content and reach their target audience.

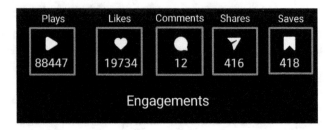

Figure. 13: Example of Engagement

a. Engagement: The algorithm takes into account engagement on the account, such as likes, comments, shares, and direct messages, to determine the relevance and popularity of the content (See the example in figure. 13).

b. Timing: The algorithm also takes into account the timing of when the post is shared. Posts that are shared when the majority of the audience is active on the platform, are more likely to be shown on the top of the feed.

c. Interest: The algorithm considers the interests of the audience, and the type of content they have engaged with in the past, to determine the relevance of the post for the audience.

d. Relationship: The algorithm also takes into account the relationship between the account and the audience, such as how long they have been following the account, and how frequently they interact with the account's content.

e. Interaction: The algorithm also considers the interactions between accounts, such as direct messages, comments, and mentions.

3. Keeping up with updates: Keeping up with updates refers to the process of staying informed about new features, changes, and best practices on Instagram, in order to optimize an account's performance and reach its target audience. Instagram is constantly evolving, and new features and updates are released regularly. Businesses need to stay up-to-date with these changes in order to make the most of the platform.

a. Research: Keeping up with updates requires research, businesses can follow Instagram's official blog and social media channels, join relevant communities and forums, and follow influencers and experts in the field to stay informed about new features and best practices.

b. Adaptation: Once new features or updates are released, businesses need to adapt their strategies and tactics accordingly, to make the most of the new opportunities.

c. Experimentation: Businesses should experiment with new features and updates as they are released, and test their effectiveness using A/B testing and other methods.

d. Analysis: Businesses should analyze the results of their experiments, and use the data to make data-driven decisions about which features and strategies to continue using, and which to discard.

e. Continuous improvement: Keeping up with updates is an ongoing process, and businesses should continuously adapt and experiment with new features and strategies in order to improve the performance of their account and reach their target audience.

4. Industry trends: Industry trends refer to the current and emerging popular practices, topics, and themes within a specific industry, such as fashion, food, travel, or technology. In the context of Instagram, industry trends refer to the types of content, hashtags, and features that are currently popular within a specific industry, and the strategies that businesses in that industry are using to reach and engage with their target audience.

a. Instagram, industry trends refer to the types of content, hashtags, and features that are currently popular within a specific industry, and the strategies that businesses in that industry are using to reach and engage with their target audience.

b. Research: Keeping up with industry trends requires research, businesses can follow Instagram accounts within their industry, join relevant communities and forums, and follow influencers and experts in the field to stay informed about popular practices, topics, and themes.

c. Adaptation: Once trends are identified, businesses need to adapt their strategies and tactics accordingly, to make the most of the new opportunities and stay relevant to their target audience.

d. Experimentation: Businesses should experiment with new trends and test their effectiveness using A/B testing and other methods.

e. Analysis: Businesses should analyze the results of their experiments and use the data to make data-driven decisions about which trends and strategies to continue using and which to discard.

f. Continuous improvement: Keeping up with industry trends is an ongoing process, and businesses should continuously adapt and experiment with new trends in order to improve the performance of their account and reach their target audience.

5. Audience insights: Audience insights refer to the process of gathering, analyzing, and understanding data about an Instagram account's target audience. The goal of audience insights is to gain a deeper understanding of the characteristics, behaviors, and needs of the target audience, in order to tailor content and messaging to better reach and convert them.

a. Data collection: Audience insights involve collecting data about the target audience, such as demographics, interests, pain points, and behaviors on Instagram. This data can be obtained from Instagram Insights, third-party analytics tools, surveys, and interviews.

b. Data analysis: Once the data is collected, it needs to be analyzed to identify patterns, trends, and insights about the target audience.

c. Personas: The data can be used to create detailed personas of the target audience, which are fictional characters that represent the different segments of the target audience.

d. Segmentation: Audience insights can also be used to segment the target audience into smaller groups with similar characteristics, behaviors, and needs.

e. Competitor analysis: Audience insights can also be used to analyze the target audience of the account's competitors, in order to identify opportunities and potential gaps in the market.

f. Actionable insights: The insights obtained from the audience analysis can be used to inform and optimize the account's content, messaging, and strategies, in order to better reach and convert the target audience.

Overall, the goal of this chapter is to provide readers with a comprehensive guide for staying up-to-date with Instagram's algorithm and features, so they can optimize their Instagram strategy and stay ahead of the competition. By utilizing the tools and strategies outlined in this chapter, readers will be able to stay current with Instagram's ever-changing landscape and adapt to new features and algorithm changes, in order to continue growing their audience and engaging with their followers.

CHAPTER 10
"The Conclusion: Building a Sustainable Instagram Kingdom"

This is an essential guide for anyone looking to establish a successful brand and monetize it on the platform. The book provides a comprehensive overview of the key strategies and techniques needed to create, grow and monetize a sustainable Instagram account. From setting up a profile that stands out, finding a niche and defining a target audience, creating engaging content, using Instagram's features to connect with the audience, and staying ahead of the game by keeping up with Instagram's algorithm and features updates. The book also covers monetization strategies such as sponsored posts, digital marketing, and product sales, as well as tips on how to measure progress and optimize the strategy over time.

Throughout the book, readers will learn how to turn their Instagram account into a profitable business by building a strong brand, reaching a large audience, and engaging with their followers. They will also learn how to track their progress, analyze their audience, and optimize their strategy over time.

The book concludes with a chapter that provides actionable steps readers can take to continue building a sustainable Instagram Kingdom and provides resources for further learning and education. Overall, Building a Brand on Instagram (from "Instagram Kingdom: Building a Brand and Making Money on Instagram") offers a clear roadmap for creating a sustainable and profitable Instagram account, by providing readers with the knowledge and tools they need to succeed on the platform. Whether you're just starting out or looking to take your existing brand to the next level, this guide is a must-read for anyone looking to build a successful and profitable Instagram Kingdom.

Bonus Tip & Tricks

1. Instagram Profile Picture:
- Aspect Ratio: 1:1
- Pixels: 110 x 110 pixels

2. Instagram Story:
- Aspect Ratio: 16:9
- Pixels: 1080 x 1920 pixels

3. Instagram Post:
- Aspect Ratio: 1:1 and 4:5
- Pixels: 1080 x 1080 pixels and 1080 x 1350 pixels

4. Instagram Carousel:
- Aspect Ratio: 1:1 and 4:5
- Pixels: 1080 x 1080 pixels and 1080 x 1350 pixels

5. Instagram Reels:
- Aspect Ratio: 9:16
- Pixels: 1080 x 1920 pixels
- Thumbnail: 1080 x 1080 pixels
- Cover: 1080 x 1920 pixels
- Frame: 1080 x 1920 pixels

- Duration: Up to 60 Seconds

6. Instagram Caption Length:
- 2,200 Characters

7. Instagram Bio:
- 150 Characters

8. Instagram Username:
- 30 Characters

9. How to increase Instagram followers: There are several ways to increase Instagram followers, including:

1. Posting regularly and consistently: This helps to keep your existing followers engaged and attracts new ones.

2. Using hashtags: This makes your posts more discoverable to people searching for content related to those hashtags.

3. Engaging with other users: This includes commenting and liking on other users' posts, as well as responding to comments on your own posts.

4. Running a promotion or contest: This can help to attract new followers and increase engagement among existing ones.

5. Collaborating with other users: This can include things like hosting a giveaway together or creating a joint post.

6. Utilizing Instagram's story feature: This can help to increase your visibility and attract new followers.

7. Optimizing your profile: This includes using a clear profile picture and bio, and including relevant links.

8. Creating a niche content: Creating a niche content and targeting the specific audience will help you to attract the right followers.

❖ Please keep in mind that building a large following on Instagram takes time and effort. It is important to be patient and to focus on creating high-quality content.

Best Wishes For You!!

I hope you enjoyed the book. If you learnt something new and found it interesting, I would be very grateful if you would consider leaving me a review with a few kind words.

➤ Feel free to ask any Queries from below options:

itsmdasif4u@gmail.com

https://instagram.com/itsmaasif

https://facebook.com/itsmaasif

https://twitter.com/itsmaasif

"Making Money on Instagram"

Coming soon in Vol. 2